Plant Adaptations

by Julie K. Lundgren

Science Content Editor:
Kristi Lew

www.rourkepublishing.com

Science content editor: Kristi Lew
A former high school teacher with a background in biochemistry and more than 10 years of experience in cytogenetic laboratories, Kristi Lew specializes in taking complex scientific information and making it fun and interesting for scientists and non-scientists alike. She is the author of more than 20 science books for children and teachers.

www.rourkepublishing.com

Photo credits: Cover © tungtopgun, Cover logo frog © Eric Pohl, test tube © Sergey Lazarev; Page 5 © Olena Mykhaylova; Page 6 © steve estvanik; Page 7 © MARGRIT HIRSCH; Page 9 © urosr; Page 10 © Roman Sigaev; Page 11 © Joao Virissimo; Page 13 © 2265524729; Page 14 © Vladimir Melnik; Page 15 © Vladimir Melnik; Page 17 © Leszek Wygachiewicz; Page 19 © irishman; Page 20 © Rechitan Sorin; Page 21 © VeryBigAlex, scoutingstock

Editor: Kelli Hicks

Cover and page design by Nicola Stratford, bdpublishing.com

Library of Congress Cataloging-in-Publication Data

Lundgren, Julie K.
 Plant adaptations / Julie K. Lundgren.
   p. cm. -- (My science library)
 Includes bibliographical references and index.
 ISBN 978-1-61741-735-1 (Hard cover) (alk. paper)
 ISBN 978-1-61741-937-9 (Sodt cover)
 1. Plants--Adaptation--Juvenile literature. I. Title.
 QK912.L86 2012
 581.4--dc22
                             2011003899

Rourke Publishing
Printed in the United States of America,
North Mankato, Minnesota
060711
060711CL

www.rourkepublishing - rourke@rourkepublishing.com
Post Office Box 643328 Vero Beach, Florida 32964

Table of Contents

Look at Plants

A plant is a living thing. Most plants can make their own food using **energy** from the Sun.

Plants make food to help them grow.

Plants can look very different. How plants look can tell us how they live.

Plants that grow in the shade may have large leaves to help them get enough sunlight.

Thorns stop most animals from munching rose bushes.

Plant Adaptations

Over time, living things change. These **adaptations** help living things **survive**.

The tallest trees get the most sunlight.

9

Cactus stems have a thick, waxy **coating**. The waxy coating slows water loss.

Cactuses can grow in hot, dry deserts.

11

Some water plants have large, flat leaves. These leaves float on the **surface** to get more sunlight.

Water lilies have adapted to living in water.

In cold places, short plants can avoid chilly winds.

Arctic plants, like the bearberry, grow close to the ground.

Over 1,500 kinds of plants survive the Arctic's short summers and poor soil.

Strange Plants, Strange Places

Plants have adapted to strange places. Some **bog** plants catch and **digest** insects to make up for poor soil **nutrients**.

Sundews are carnivorous plants. They trap insects in a sweet, sticky gel.

Not all plants live on the ground. Some grow on treetops. They get water from rain or the air.

Rainforest trees often have other plants, such as bromeliads, growing on their branches.

bromeliads

19

Plants have different looks and ways of living. Look at plants to learn how they live.

Plants grow almost everywhere. Some plants even grow under water.

SHOW What You Know

1. What are some ways plants adapt to where they live?

2. Why do you think some cactuses have spines or prickles?

3. Look at the plants in your neighborhood. How have they adapted to living in your area?

Glossary

adaptations (ad-ap-TAY-shunz): changes over time that help living things survive

bog (BOG): wet, mossy land with few soil nutrients

coating (KOH-ting): a layer covering something

digest (dye-JEST): to break down food so it can be used by the body

energy (EN-ur-jee): the ability to do work or make a process happen, as the Sun fuels food-making in plants

nutrients (NOO-tree-uhnts): minerals and other substances in the soil that are needed by plants to stay healthy and grow

surface (SER-fuss): the outside or outermost layer of something, like the top of a body of water

survive (sur-VIVE): to continue to live, in spite of dangers

Index

Websites

http://urbanext.illinois.edu/gpe/case1/c1facts1b.html

http://water.epa.gov/type/wetlands/bog.cfm

www.cotf.edu/ete/modules/msese/earthsysflr/adapt.html

www.ftexploring.com/me/photosyn1.html

www.mbgnet.net/bioplants/adapt.html

www.tooter4kids.com/Plants/parts_of_plants.htm

About the Author

Julie K. Lundgren grew up near Lake Superior where she liked to muck about in the woods, pick berries, and expand her rock collection. Her interests led her to a degree in biology. She lives in Minnesota with her family.

24